SUPPORT
SAVE
SUPPLY

SUPPORT
SAVE
SUPPLY

Rob Bailey

Airlife England

ACKNOWLEDGEMENTS

The following persons kindly provided the photographs that
made this book possible:

FS C. L. Bogg
Flt Lt W. M. Colquhoun
Flt Lt C. D. Cranstoun
Jeremy Flack — Aviation Photographs International
Flt Lt D. Fry
Flt Lt K. Hartland
Flt Lt S. McCarthy
SAC McIvor
Gp Capt C. J. Morris
Flt Lt N. P. Moxon
M Eng A. Muniandy
Flt Lt M. Murphy
Cpl J. A. Osborough
M Eng S. P. Ponting
Fg Off J. Skinner
Flt Lt M. J. White
Flt Lt N. J. Young

First published in the UK in 1992 by

Airlife Publishing Ltd.

British Library Cataloguing in Publication Data

A Catalogue record of this book is available from the British
Library

ISBN 1 85310 321 7

Printed by Livesey Ltd., Shrewsbury.

Airlife Publishing Ltd

101 Longden Road, Shrewsbury, SY3 9EB, England.

For RAF Lyneham, the RAF's Hercules base OPERATION GRANBY started on the night of the 8 August 1990, when aircraft, crews, support personnel and equipment where positioned at RAF Akrotiri, Cyprus to establish a slip pattern whilst plans were agreed for the destinations of the men and equipment in the Gulf Area.

Below: RAF Lyneham's operations room comprises elements of Engineering, Supply, Air Movements and Operations staffs to co-ordinate and manage over 60 Hercules of the RAF's Air Transport Fleet.

Opposite: Assorted freight for Dhahran is loaded by Henley fork lift trucks.

Below: In case of rapid de-pressurisation or smoke and fumes in the aircraft, the Hercules has an emergency oxygen system. The oxygen is provided by converting liquid oxygen (LOX) into a gas. The replenishment of LOX is a dangerous and skilful task carried out by engineering staff prior to a sortie deploying to the Gulf.

Below: The enhanced 'Watchman' radar enabled Lyneham Air Traffic controllers to co-ordinate safely the hourly departures and arrivals of Hercules aircraft to the numerous destinations both within the UK and overseas.

Opposite: To enable the engineers to meet the demand for airframes and to ensure aircraft remained in a serviceable state, additional engineering personel were drafted into Lyneham from such places as St. Athan, Benson and Abingdon.

Opposite: 'Stretching' the Mk. 3 Hercules extended the freight bay by only 15 feet but increased the capacity by 30%. The most common floor configuration for freight is roller conveyor with side guidance, enabling palletized loads to be on and off loaded rapidly.

Below: Priority was given to the out loading of ammunition to all fighter and ground attack aircraft bases throughout the Middle East.

Overleaf: A desert camouflaged Hercules Mk.1 stands on the pan at Lyneham next to a standard camouflaged 'stretched' Mk. 3 Hercules.

Opposite: Loading Heavylift Canadair CL 44 Guppy at Lyneham with assorted freight for the Gulf.

Below: The Alliance provided additional airlift support for the outloading of freight. A Spanish Hercules being loaded at Lyneham for a destination in the Gulf.

Opposite: The 'Big Green Bags' weighing over 70lb became a familiar sight as crews embarked on their aircraft.

Below: To be prepared for all eventualities and with the prospect of Nuclear, and Biological and Chemical warfare a reality, crews carried war stocks of NBC clothing and equipment on all sorties.

Opposite: Puma Helicopters of 33 and 230 Squadrons are dismantled and air freighted to the Gulf for logistic support and casualty evacuation where they were later painted in Pink camouflage.

Below: A pilot fully equipped in NBC clothing with a portable ventilator is afforded complete protection from Nuclear, Biological or Chemical attack. This pilot is also able to operate at low level at night with the aid of his night vision goggles. (NVGs).

Overleaf: A C130 Mk.1 flown by a crew from 24 Squadron arrives in the Gulf with 20,000lb of freight having flown nearly 3000 miles.

Opposite: A C130 en route from Qaisumah to Al Jubail along the 'pipe line' route – some 180 miles of straight road and oil pipe lines.

Below: A Flight Engineer carrying out his pre-flight checks which includes all flying controls, radios, electrics and hydraulic systems. In flight he is responsible for fuel management and fault diagnosis in consultation with the pilots.

Opposite: On 30 October 1990, three Hercules aircraft and six crews, plus engineering, air movements and support personnel from RAF Lyneham deployed to Riyadh's King Khaled International Airport (KKIA) to set up an Air Transport Detachment (AT Det).

Below: To assist with the rapid turn-round of aircraft, the local Saudi fuel company refuelled the Hercules at KKIA.

Opposite: On 23 December 1990, two Hercules of the Royal New Zealand Air Force (RNZAF) together with three crews and supporting personnel arrived to join the AT Det. The crews were from 40 Squadron based at Whenuapi, Auckland. In mid-January 1991 the detachment was expanded to four crews. RAF Mk. 3, RNZAF Mk. 1 Hercules join French AF Transell and KC135 aircraft at Riyadh.

Below: The initial basis for the tasking of the AT Det was using the 'Hub and Spoke' principle. RAF Tristar and VC10 aircraft fed the 'Hub' at KKIA with freight and passengers.

Opposite: Gulf locations included Seeb and Thumrait in Oman, Minhad in the United Arab Emirates.

Below: and Saudi Arabian airfields such as Dhahran, Tabuk, Jubail and Qaisumah.

Opposite: Flying back from the north west area around Tabuk not all the desert was sand.

Below: Flying routes to the east of Riyadh would always reveal hundreds of camels wandering aimlessly in the desert with the ever attentive Nomad in modern day transport – the pick-up truck.

Overleaf: Whilst the AT Det at Riyadh was fully occupied the remainder of the Hercules fleet operated to and from the UK and Germany as well as the British Sovereign base in Cyprus.

Below: From Cyprus the aircraft would fly direct to the Gulf and return in support of other Royal Air Force squadrons or the British Armoured Division. Troops would be off-loaded at Al Jubail to travel by road to their units further up country.

Opposite: The Air Loadmaster overseeing the off-loading of a CVRT at Jubail.

Opposite: A Mk. 1 operated by a crew from LXX Squadron en route to Dhahran with munitions for Tornado F3s.

Below: The featureless desert made low level navigation difficult as most electronic navigation aids had been switched off.

Opposite: The aircraft commander's cupola in the roof proved invaluable for spotting other aircraft and provides 360° vision.

Below: Flying at 250' above the ground, the windows soon got obliterated by insects thus the look out for other aircraft was made more difficult. After each sortie the air engineer was meticulous with the cleaning of windows, in particular the cupola.

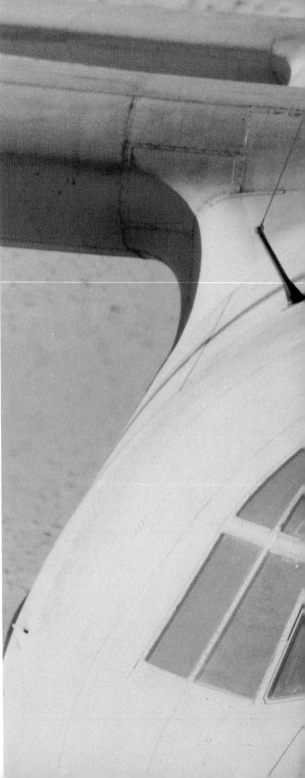

Opposite: Aircraft newly arrived in theatre were given 'Desert Pink' camouflage. There were no spray shop facilities available.

Below: Desert Pink had to be applied by hand with rollers and paint brush. The colour was particularly effective at low level.

Opposite: Crews practised rapid climb techniques to avoid ground fire.

Below: Looking down at a Hercules the desert camouflage made it
difficult to be seen by enemy aircraft.

Opposite: Shortly after the start of the air war on 15 January 1991, the AT Det came under fire from Scud missiles which were successfully intercepted by Patriot missiles. It is interesting to note that this SCUD brought down near Riyadh has instructions in English.

Below: The Hercules was used for ground troops to develop evasive tactics should they be atttacked by enemy aircraft. The variable speeds of the Hercules at low level could simulate a variety of aircraft and helicopters.

Overleaf: At the start of Desert Storm, the AT Det's main role was the air evacuation of casualties from the field hospitals at Qaisumah and Al Jubail to Riyadh. The Hercules was fitted with 30 stretchers and could carry an additional 40 wounded, together with medical support teams drawn from No 1 Aeromedical Evacuation Squadron (RAF Lyneham) and 4626 Aeromedical Squadron .

Below: Porton Liners provided decontamination units and operating theatres that could function during a chemical attack. They were located underneath the Hercules detachment in the terminal at KKIA.

Opposite: Ground engineer support at KKIA was limited only by the basic facilities available, but proved highly successful. Over 2300 sorties were flown with the loss of only three, and they were due to bad weather. Members of RAF Lyneham Engineering Wing making sure the aircraft servicing log book was kept current and correct.

Below: Casualty off-load - members of 4626 Aeromed Squadron practising the on and off load of stretcher casualties in the intense heat at Al Jubail Field Hospital.

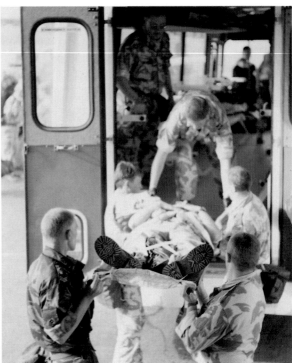

Opposite: Following the augmentation of first and second line engineering staffs at Lyneham, the average daily offer of aircraft to the Joint Headquarters was 35.

Below: The overwing inspection of fuel tanks was vital to ensure that fuel gauges were reading correctly and that tanks were full, particularly as some flights were flown almost to the limit of the aircraft's fuel endurance.

Opposite: The average monthly flying rate was 90 hours per crew member. Although many aircrew flew in excess of the normal peacetime limit of 120 hours in any 28-day period, no-one exceeded the 'operational' limit of 150 hours. The maximum crew duty day experienced was 25 hours.

Below: Wheeled vehicles of 7 Armoured Brigade arrive in the Gulf. Three Land-Rovers and trailers can be carried in a Mk. 3 Hercules.

Overleaf: Composite Rations (Compo) being off-loaded by a Henley Forklift. Note the ramp support that is used when palletized loads are in use.

Opposite: August proved to be the busiest month on record for the Lyneham Hercules Wing. The previous highest flying total was in May 1982 during Operation Corporate (Falklands Campaign) when 6800 hours was achieved. In August 1990 over 8259 hours were flown, representing 1.9 million miles and 4.0 million gallons of fuel; 3.2 million pounds of freight was moved, together with 2547 passengers and 288 vehicles. A co-pilot from 30 Squadron makes an approach to Seeb after a six-hour flight from Cyprus.

Above: Initially, the Royal Air Force was tasked to harass enemy airfield operations rather than attempt to close a selected few. In the early days of the war, Tornado GRIs carried out low-level attacks with JP233 to crater runways or taxiways.

Opposite: The RAF's Air Transport Force flew a total of 50,000 hours in support of Operation Granby, with 40,100 hours being completed by RAF Lyneham Hercules.

Below: Outsize loads such as Challenger Tank Repair Vehicles, Main Base Transfer Loaders and Aircraft Towing Tractors had to be carried in civilian chartered aircraft. An Antonov AN 124 Transport aircraft on the pan at Riyadh, having delivered mobile medical units to the Field Hospital.

Opposite: Sandstorms could develop quickly and make visual approaches into Qaisumah almost impossible for Hercules casevac crews. A mobile Surveillance Radar was provided by the Americans and was housed in the back of a heavy duty vehicle.

Below: Makeshift taxiways for casevac aircraft at Al Jubail Field Hospital were achieved by Combat Armoured Tractors.

Overleaf: At 0100 hours on 24 February 1991, the Coalition Ground Forces attacked the Iraqi Army. The 1st British Armoured Division knocked out over 300 enemy tanks, taking 8,000 prisoners and advanced 180 miles in just four days' fighting. To ensure that the Army was re-supplied rapidly with combat supplies, including ammunition, food and water, the Hercules used desert 'strips' which were built by the Royal Engineers. The strips, some 3,000 feet in length, required skill to locate and land on them.

Below: The technique of positive landing is adopted for strips due to their short length.

Opposite: The propellers are put into reverse thrust by altering their blade angle, which effectively brings the aircraft to a stop in a short distance. Over use of reverse has to be avoided otherwise the cockpit is engulfed in dust and sand, and all forward visibility lost.

Opposite: Constant use of 'strips' or LZs (Landing Zones) soon makes them rutted. The Royal Engineers either re-roll them or, if they are too badly damaged, build a new one.

Below: The sharp stones on LZs quickly tear and damage the tyres, Despite their pressure, the tyre bay was kept constantly busy inspecting and fitting new tyres.

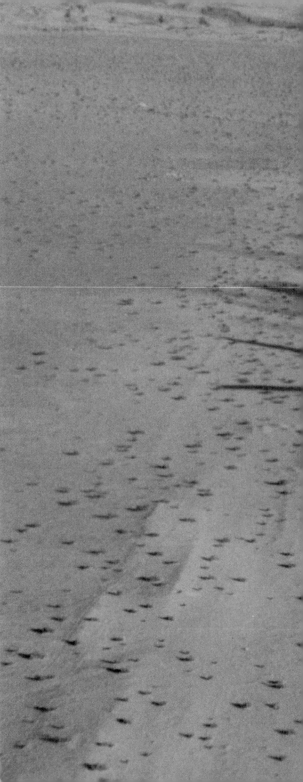

Opposite: As well as damaging tyres, the stones and sand thrown up on LZs quickly 'sandblasted' the hand-painted desert camouflage. Aircraft prepared for strip work have the under-belly aerials removed or protected and special reinforced landing lights fitted.

Below: To ensure there are no problems re-starting engines or the need for generators at LZs, all off-loads and on-loads are carried out with engines in low speed, ground idle. In addition, this keeps the ground time to an absolute minimum. Vehicles of 7 Armoured Brigade being loaded whilst XV 297 keeps its engines running.

Opposite: The ladies of RAF Lyneham set up a 'Gulf Line' for the 370 detached Lyneham personnel. Their parcels of goodies helped tremendously to keep up the morale of the airmen and women deployed in areas where basic necessities were difficult to obtain.

Below: To provide extra security whilst handling Iraqi prisoners of war, dogs of the RAF Police Dog Section, RAF Lyneham, were deployed to the forward areas in the Gulf.

Overleaf: To enable a short take-off distance from a desert strip, a 'Tac Rotate' speed as low as 85 knots can be used with 18,000lb of torque set on each engine.

Below: During the build-up and throughout the Gulf War, air-to-air refuelling played a major part in the success of the air war. A total of nine VC10Ks of No 101 Squadron, together with one or two TriStar K1s of No 216 Squadron, were in constant use and were operated alongside the Hercules at Riyadh.

Opposite: The aircraft is fitted with a UHF-Homer which operates on 243.0 MHz — the military emergency frequency. It helps locate personnel or aircraft and ships by giving a Left or Right indication, and when centralized the active beacon is easily found.

Opposite: Toyota pick-ups doubled as crew transport and engineers' runarounds at Riyadh.

Below: The C130 Hercules is affectionately called 'Fat Albert' by most operators of the aircraft. The Riyadh Hercules detachment soon nicknamed it 'Albert of Arabia'.

Opposite: On 28 February, RAF Lyneham's Hercules were the first coalition fixed wing aircraft to land at Kuwait International Airport since the Iraqi occupation in August 1990. With a southerly wind, locating the airfield visually was hampered by the thick, dense smoke of the burning oilfields. The smoke extended from 150 feet above the ground to over 10,000 feet.

Below: Members of Lyneham's Mobile Air Movements Squadron processed over 23,000 passengers and handled over 20.3 million pounds of freight at Riyadh. Manifesting passengers and freight is vital in keeping track of individuals and each piece of freight.

Opposite: The whole of the airport had suffered from wanton destruction — many of the buildings harboured booby traps.

Below: The keys to the British Embassy were taken on the first flight into Kuwait, whilst on the second, the British Ambassador returned to the Embassy. Later flights took the Prime Minister, Mr John Major, and the Secretary of State for Defence, Mr Tom King.

Opposite: With all-round Air Traffic Control facilities totally destroyed, the in-bound Hercules were dependent on the detachment of Royal Signals and RAF Tactical Comms Wing for the passage of information, such as wind direction, pressure settings and the base of the smoke.

Below: A small team of Mobile Air Movements (MAMs) personnel were deployed to Kuwait International and Army vehicles were used for a multitude of purposes, including an unusual 'Follow Me'.

Opposite: The dense, oily smoke caused problems on aircraft windows and the airframes themselves; it left a very thin viscose coating all over. The engineers removed it by using a detergent sprayed on at high pressure.

Below: At night, the extent of the burning oil wells became more apparent. From the aircraft pans, over 200 fires were visible.

Opposite: For the next two months a daily schedule operated from Riyadh to Kuwait, transporting men and equipment into and out of the theatre of operations. A pink Hercules, crewed by members of 47 Squadron, returns to Riyadh at low level.

Below: XV 178, taxying into Jubail some 200 miles south of Kuwait. The smoke from the burning oilfields darkens the sky and caused the air temperature to drop by 10°C.

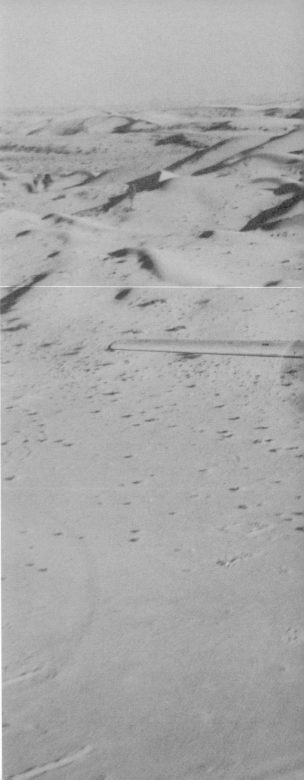

Opposite: The announcement to withdraw troops and equipment as soon as possible was met with great relief. Heavy Movements machinery was positioned at Kuwait International to help load equipment from the forward Division Area to airheads at Al Jubail and Dhahran for the Tristars and VC10s to return to the UK. Note the unofficial return of 'Royal Air Force Middle East' after an absence of over fifteen years.

Below: The daily tote board in the AT Det Operations room for 4 March 1991 reveals interesting statistics for a detachment of only seven RAF and two RNZAF Hercules and a total of eighteen crews. The Pax, or Passengers, does include those carried by the Tristars and VC10s!

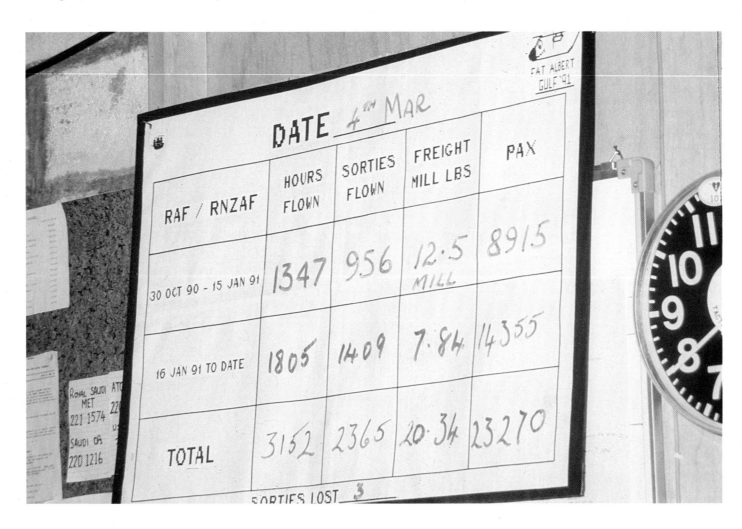

RAF / RNZAF	HOURS FLOWN	SORTIES FLOWN	FREIGHT MILL LBS	PAX
30 OCT 90 – 15 JAN 91	1347	956	12·5 MILL	8915
16 JAN 91 TO DATE	1805	1409	7·84	14355
TOTAL	3152	2365	20·34	23270

DATE 4TH MAR

FAT ALBERT GULF '91

SORTIES LOST 3

Opposite: Equipment that could not withstand the rigours of a large sea voyage were air lifted from the forward areas and transferred to UK-bound Tristars at Riyadh. A Mk. 1 Hercules with minimum fuel on board to enable maximum freight to be carried, takes off from an LZ north of Kuwait.

Below: Before any personnel were repatriated, those killed in action were returned first. RAF Lyneham had the honour of flying home the bodies as a Hercules could best complete the task, although Brize Norton was the selected terminal. The ceremonial on the ground was carried out by the staff of the London Garrison with contingents from all three Services providing a guard of honour; the bearer parties came from the appropriate regiments

Opposite: March 15 — Comic Relief Day. XV 305 had its nose painted red and was towed along the taxiways to raise money for charity. In the Gulf, crews received their red noses via the Gulf Line. A composite crew from Staneval, 242 OCU and 47 Squadron stand in front of an Iraqi ZSU 234, suitably dressed with their red noses.

Below: During the Gulf War the Hercules — the work horse of most air forces — could be seen throughout the area. A C130 of the Royal Australian Air Force awaits its next task. The white upper fuselage and cockpit helped to reduce the freight bay and flight deck temperature whilst in the Gulf and when at its base at Richmond Air Base, near Sydney, Australia.

Opposite: Equally popular was aircraft nose art. The Second World War habit of painting bathing beauties or cartoons was adopted by the Lyneham ground crew based in Riyadh. At one time, all seven aircraft were decorated but because of in-depth engineering requirements the aircraft were rotating almost weekly. One of the first to appear was XV 215 with the 'Fat Slags'.

Below: The withdrawal of troops was planned at 1,000 per day, which meant at least thirty-five days of heavy airlift for the Hercules.

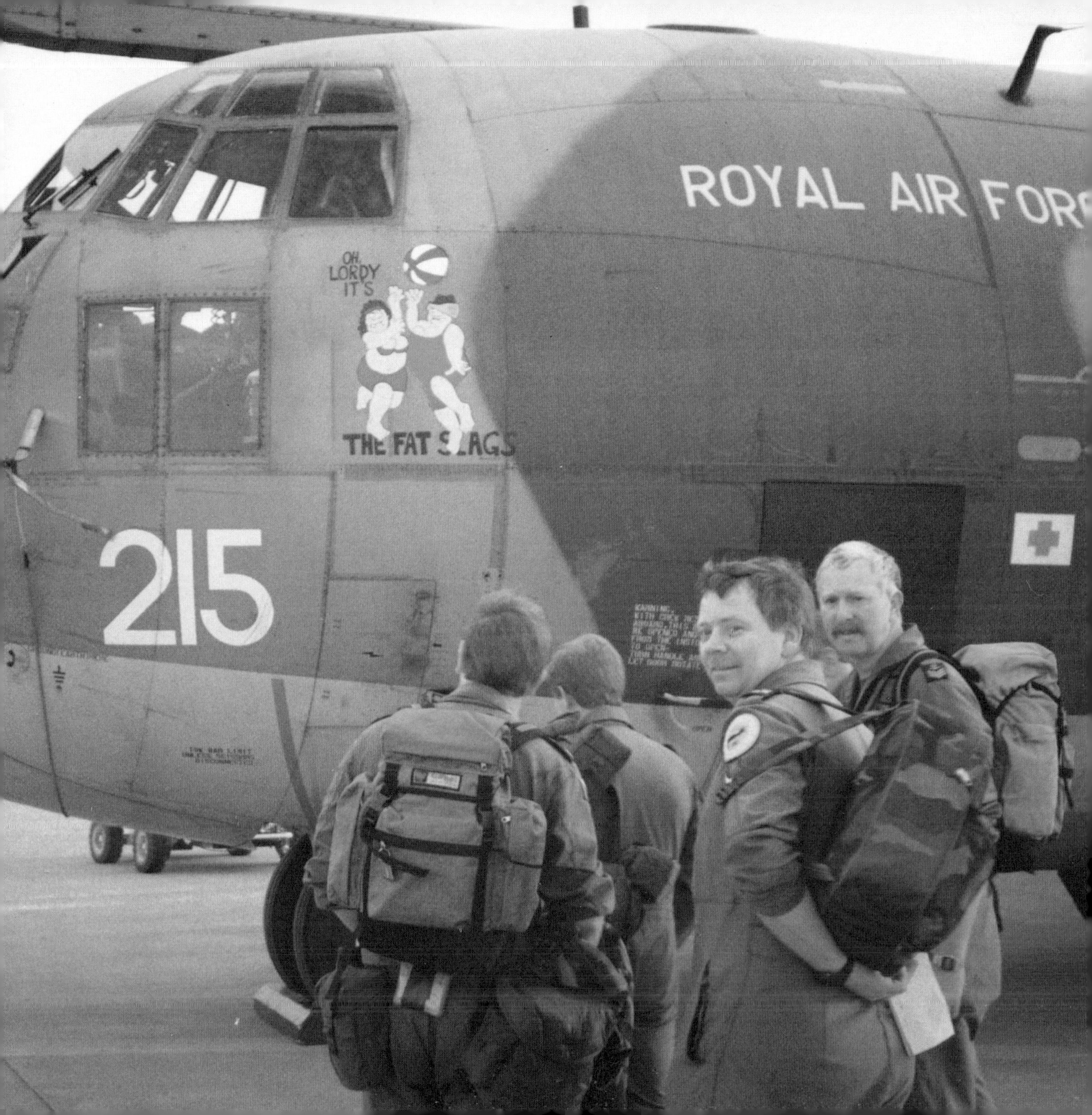
ROYAL AIR FORC
OH, LORDY IT'S
THE FAT SLAGS
215

Opposite: Early versions of the 'Foxy Lady' on XV 206 appeared naked, but to save any embarrassment she was told to get her bikini on.

Below: XV 306 of 'B' line proved popular with the Red Baron.

Opposite and below: Colourful Garfield contrasted with the black and white Dennis the Menace on XV 292.

ROYAL AIR F
LET ME AT HIM!
DENNIS THE MENNACE
02
WARNING.
WITH CREW MEMBERS
ABOARD, THIS DOOR WILL
BE OPENED AND CLOSED
FROM THE INSIDE ONLY
TO OPEN-
TURN HANDLE AND
LET DOOR ROTATE DOWN

Opposite: An American C130 had nose art that may have been an indication of the type of freight it was carrying.

Below: To save any further embarrassment, 'Betty Boobs' was painted on the crew entrance door and was thus not visible when the aircraft was parked with the crew door open.

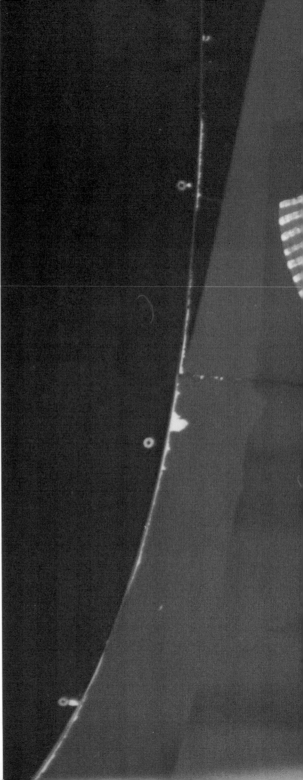

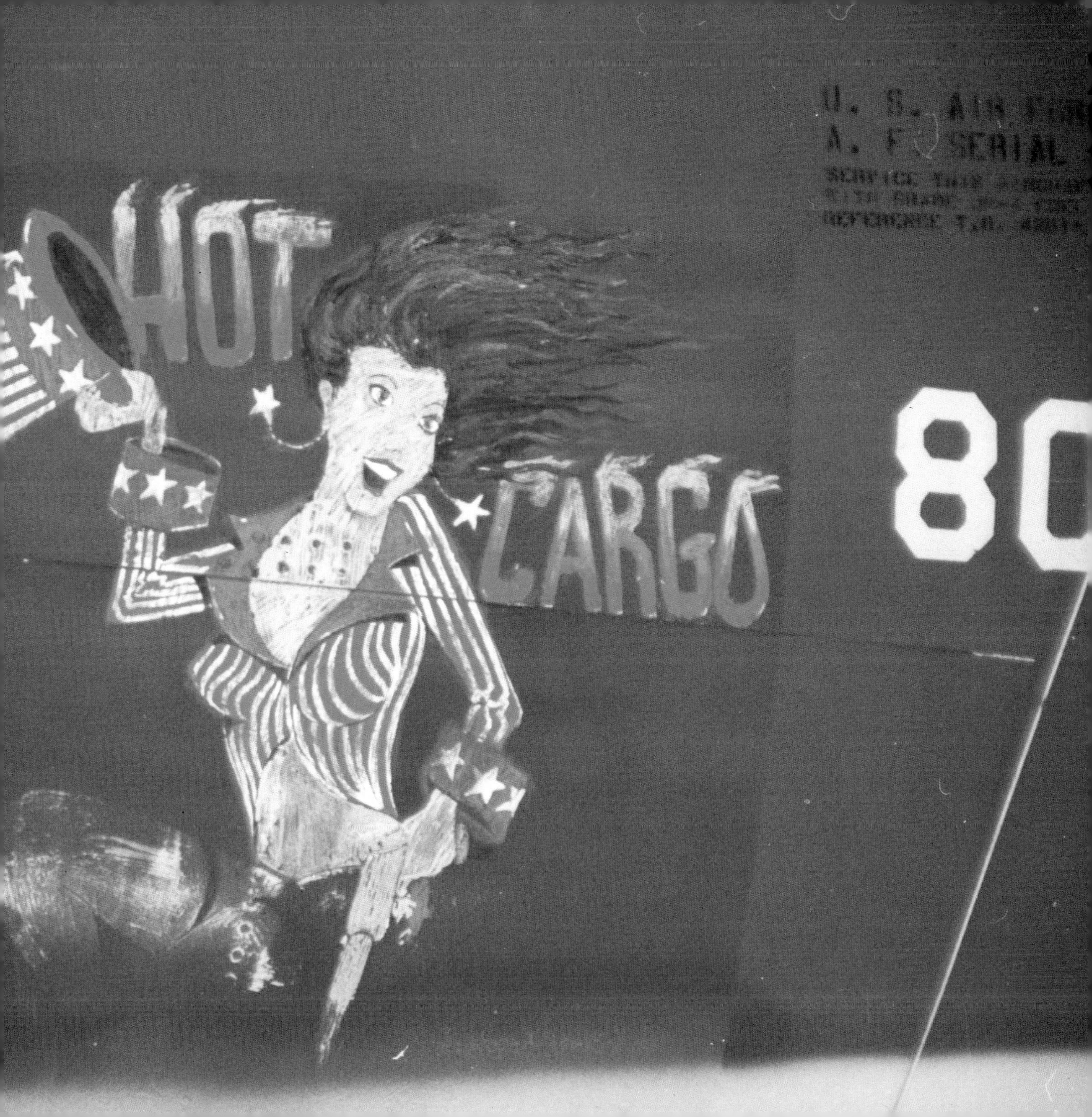

U. S. AIR
A. F. SERIAL
HOT
CARGO
80

Opposite: The withdrawal of troops from all Gulf locations continued apace. Fat Albert was a welcome sight to those who had been living in the desert for months.

Below: An American AC-130 displays its lethal 'cargo' by its nose art.

Opposite: Whilst the return of all elements of the British Forces continued throughout March and April, the plight of the Kurdish refugees in Northern Iraq received considerable media coverage.

Below: A C130 of the United Arab Emirates at Kuwait International helping with the carriage of freight and passengers to the main airheads.

Below: On 4 April, RAF Lyneham executives were asked to consider the operational implications of air dropping supplies to the Kurds. On the 6 April, it was announced on the national radio that the RAF was about to begin airdrops into Northern Iraq. Following a period of intensive planning, the first relief aircraft departed from Lyneham for Turkey at 0009 hrs that night. Wg. Cdr. C. J. Morris, OC LXX Sqn., the AT Det. Cdr. briefing crews from LXX and 47 Sqn. about the inaccessible areas being considered for dropping zones (DZs). This was the start of operation Provide Comfort.

Opposite: The relief organisation was mainly driven by the Americans with mixed force packages of USAF, RAF and French Air Force transport aircraft being launched from Adana Incirlik, Turkey. Due to the uncertainty of Iraq air and ground fire operational sorties were flown under an umbrella of supporting aircraft including F15, F16, F4G, A10, EF111, EC130, MC 130, HC130, MH53, E3 and KC135. An A10 formates on a RAF C130 shortly after take-off from Incirlik.

Opposite: Each RAF C130 Mk.1 was loaded with 16 one-ton containers which were dropped in multiples of four as the drop zones were not large enough to accommodate a stick of containers. The drops were carried out at 140 Kts at 6000' above mean sea level.

Below: Members of 47 Air Dispatch Squadron (Royal Corps of Transport) based at RAF Lyneham preparing loads of 'Composite Rations' and sleeping bags for aerial delivery to the Kurds.

Opposite: Successful drops during Operation Provide Comfort were painted on the fuselage. In this instance the aircraft has dropped over 320 tons of supplies.

Below: The drop zones (DZs) were small and often close to the refugees' tents. The accuracy of drops was imperative. In this valley the DZ is centre right on sloping ground.

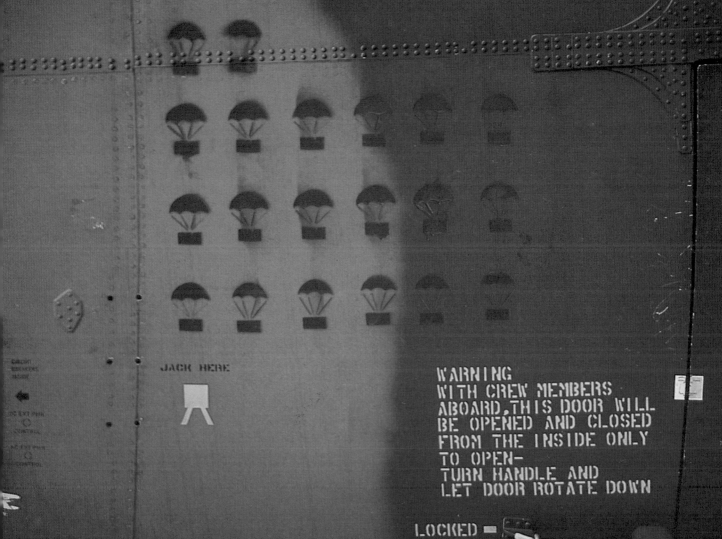

JACK HERE

WARNING
WITH CREW MEMBERS
ABOARD, THIS DOOR WILL
BE OPENED AND CLOSED
FROM THE INSIDE ONLY
TO OPEN-
TURN HANDLE AND
LET DOOR ROTATE DOWN

LOCKED

OPEN

E

A political settlement was reached over the future of the Kurds and so the RAFs contribution to Operation Provide Comfort finished on 1 May 1991, and crews returned to the UK. The final Hercules departed from the Gulf at the end of Operation Granby on 16 June 1991.